Barbarism

Also by Molly McQuade

An Unsentimental Education
Stealing Glimpses: Of Poetry, Poets, and Things in Between
By Herself

Barbarism

Molly McQuade

FOUR WAY BOOKS

Marshfield

Editorial Office
Four Way Books
P.O. Box 607
Marshfield, MA 02050
www.gypsyfish.com/fourway

Library of Congress
Catalog Card Number: 99-71364

ISBN 1-884800-27-0

Cover painting, "Archaeopteryx:
The First Bird," by Rudolf Freund,
by permission of Eleonore Freund.

Book Design: Henry Israeli

This book is manufactured in the United States of America and
printed on acid-free paper.

Four Way Books is a division of Friends of Writers, Inc., a Vermont-
based not-for-profit organization. We are grateful for the assistance
we receive from individual donors and private foundations.

ACKNOWLEDGMENTS

The author thanks the editors of the following publications, in which some of the poems in this book first appeared, at times with different titles or in slightly different form:

The American Scholar: "Egret"

Ellipsis: "Congregating"

Fence: "Care"

Green Mountains Review: "Noon"

Lit: "Pine Barrens"

The Massachusetts Review: "The Law" and "Just a Crimp in Lushness"

Michigan Quarterly Review: **"Mouse History"**

New Letters: "January Calm"

The Paris Review: "Bondage"

Parnassus: "Bees Stumble" and "My Belugas"

Pequod: "Archaic Corn"

Salamander: "Clematis"

Virginia Quarterly Review: "Belief" and "Queen Anne's Lace"

Western Humanities Review: "Fossil Knowledge"

The author also gratefully acknowledges the assistance and support of the following in the writing of this book: the Pew Charitable Trusts, the New York Foundation for the Arts, the MacDowell Colony, the Ucross Foundation, the Squaw Valley Community of Writers, and the Wesleyan Writers Conference.

CONTENTS

I

BARBARISM

Every day, a new web
is left for me, to dry by seven,
heaped up, hard to scan,
a gummy stocking. The radial swish
is shocking to my eye,
my touch; each time
I stumble, try
to hush the mesh.
Spiders don't keep anything,
vanish with their baggy juices
before I can remember what morning is.
I'd rather stop waking for weeks,
neglect so as to desire better,
discover,
although no spider has ever had to learn—
her craft in spinning was decided
before she was born. Designs transpire.
This one hangs in the door, fluttering
with loop-de-loop drool.
Looking, I think: city. Its streets are coarse.
I think, Armani. Faceted cling
and unusual stripes.
And I think, there's a vacancy
in this flat nest.
The spider did it and ran.
She forgot to put the postage stamp on. She was protuberant
in a thin hammock
that couldn't bear her vague spots.
Yet I like to picture her,
unwelcome artist scuttling on a strand
and vowing to create a disturbance.
She hurts the apparatus
as an iron can ruin ruffles.
A barbarism is inside us.

MURKY SWAN

Earth is testing us
to see how far we're filled.
The drenching is tedious. The swan
must be very cold.
She knits a white fiber
that doesn't belong to her,
kneading and working her insuperable shoulders
in dip and lull.
Her bill strokes like a cello bow,
niggling between feathers,
and she would never think of leaving
such a long sonata
of streaming isolation, lengthening
as sounds pat bay water beside her
and lift unseemly into mist-strewn air.
The large, vague, reticulate feet
are chaffing her runway loveliness;
her squat end, trying not to sink,
feathers a buoyant, beautiful triangle.
Her innerness lingers,
a diamonded, precise rhythm
of slick frond in that portal.
Secrecy softens such intimate parts,
and one suspects perfection
in the whorl unseen
of a knockout on a lake.
The bold and stormy body
will harbor it
until she sighs, floating off.
I want you
with a white clingingness and fury.
The swan must be very cold.

CARE

You want to be cared for?
  The way the fox wraps its pitted,
lank tail around the cold char of its body?
  Or as it happens to fishes,
stroked by sheer, sleek currents?
  Is the sensing sudden, or a lush succumbing,
plum swoon, pearly listlessness?
  Twined talons of a starfish attend me,
flung rock made desperate
  in a long abominable drift, waiting,
and you might be a pelican
  sagging with spent flight,
empty jowl reeking,
  wings slack with grit.
Below you, twisted agate,
  I entreat the dropped mussels,
provide you with a subtle footing
  as tide slithers back.
My mouth has eaten sky
  but I am starving,
always almost senseless;
  I tire, dream of the starfish.
Each digit suckles with sleepless, grasping ends
  that cling to substance as our cells
are said to seize themselves, but don't
  with so much else to confront them:
blood fjords grazing forests of anemone,
  wizard pods protecting the ravaged inner distance,
instincts rolling by, fluffy white.
  The body blanches, tingles, squeezes;
you try to live in it
  without me, planet's germ,
little innocent, fury.

I would comb the toss of river in the harm
you promise, ferry embolism,
    lie in lightning underneath your eyes;
slip between pain and callus.
    Care is like a rotting. Hear my heat:
it addles, loses, tightens.

BREEDING

They breed themselves, spendthrift, without help.
The tops have a tiff with the stalks
and start to let themselves out.
It happens once, a weak chord, a squeaked note,
and as the fern stoops to unfold,
the fiber groans in a song of sunstruck defiance
and want. Self-envelopment, self-desire, stun
with warmth, and the fern forgets
the life before light hit.
Comes a spasm of stealth abandoned,
underwater chucked, then that arch
with the wadded-up green circus in it,
coded, clenched. Consuming. Every fern does it,
maiden, heated, sired by itself—
springs up.

II

TOOLS

You must farm your anger. You'll need tools.
The ones flecked with rust on the seams may be the best
for your survival,
salted with sea, rain, tears.
They know the elements already,
only need your chastening hand.
So temper them.
Work until the wood and metal twinge,
a hard sugar,
an intelligent plain.
Yet remember, your way
must be wholesome,
a decorum,
and crisp in its silence,
edged simple.
When you hear the silence, listen again,
then mound it,
a weather incurable in your palm.
Don't delay.
Don't deform.
For there is no doubting the exigence or usefulness
of anger,
smooth as it seems.
It is different from the wayward feelings that molest us—
their yields are trickling.
Leave them behind.
The trouble comes when anger is not known
or when, a dubious bargainer,
it is half seen.
Hard enough to enter the dark
without anger also freezing your nape;
hard enough to swell muscle without
the meat of anger mixing in.

But then,
why are words gentle?
They farm the fury they own.
They finish it
with slippery pleasure,
harmless,
or with the harm done.

SEEKING AN ORCHID

Seeking an orchid, I think: she must be a mistake,
an extreme unlived with—

a goner,
foul arctic from Cuba,
her fiber almost extinct,

flame advisor to night.

Her lavender shroud,
inked cheek;
the wound rendered and kept—

an ancient pretender no less efficient
for being a zooish survivor
of an old earth.

None of her number seems very abundant.
Rain can't make it better
for the fresh, the skinless,
suckered or pure,
twinned with fang, as she is.

Her demurral—ripe.
The deep bit her,
leaving a sink.

LAVISH DISENCHANTMENT

Pink peonies, languishing in bunches
like worn, amorous bodies,
are bedraggling the avenue
with all-out wiltedness,
the rapture of doing what you want
until you are not
and some body whimpers in harvest
and there is nothing to add but a deepening blush
at the tip of petal or brain
in protest of having to be flesh or flower
and having to let go.
Pink does not begrudge, can't,
the color must show what is in and under it,
hearkening now
to whatever comes next—
the bicyclist, steaming into his own exultance;
leery tilt of foxglove;
antique surge of bonsai.
Among these, peonies
alone seem done for
like partnerless coquettes
listless at a concert,
and they are all lain down now
in some merchant's bin,
regretting it
with crimps and snuffles,
lavish disenchantment.

THE SHARP TOUCH

A gray lichen slips around a root near woods,
and peach trees hover dark pink,
torch up, splinters
of bark,
down the dull road that takes us,
sinks,
webs off with blue rot.

The peach's sharp touch would be a warning
to the fox aglaze in the nest with winning
out hot births
from their syrups;
a danger in streaky winds.

All thorn, the tree tears at a sky
filled with bodies,
swollen, aglut, flotsam, March, grief
in ice as earth must change, always;
jammed with starlings,
hit with silence,
shambles, nothing to show
but seeds; a low fungus beside the grass
galled to grow up—

Poor in the dark as birds pierce bark,
restless and fast and sure;

Knocked on as another rain leaves us.

The tree would purge the long wounds among the hills
holding the last of snow,
the dark of dead, the large,
flawed bed of the old
deep in rustling, leaned on rock,
limp with ferns just let up;

The season hurts her.

FOX

She wants to do the unforgivable
and be unforgiven over and over,
but to do what she must,
she has to devise it. And she doesn't know how,
what it is or what it could be,
how exactly to name it, kill it. Actually,
she is guileless,
and her power is shabby and strange to her.
But every act is a sabotage
of something or someone, an excitement,
a betrayal, blood in the wind,
secreted so as to be snuck and swallowed. And she will obey
this blood, raise her nose to find it.
Still, all her life of common senses—gloom, green,
slime, silence—has not prepared her
for this, not spelled the word
that reeks and calls to her. "Unforgivable":
what the squirrel would not covet
with its glossy tail
or little fever-nose.
(The frivolous will not travel here.)
The unforgivable: a pheasant blinks in fear before it,
bobs, glistens,
and scuttles. There is no knowing this nature we share,
squeezing us
with a shivery shawl of moth-life,
full-bodied and drear. She listens, snares the shifty cloth
with her brown teeth
and aching muzzle,
thanks the large beetle for stirring her this once
with its barge of muddle, woebegone and tender—
but it won't matter.
She wants to slink down and further,

along the winding foot-pass
by the oaks,
stooped, rutted. She wants no one to see her
but the gnats who doze and drown in her rumor
of salt, heat, and fur.
She wants, with her nose, to savage
the owls in their fluffy keeps
who smugly can survive
a reputation for wildness.

SEED, RANKLING

Bilge-baby, you look like something's gone terribly wrong:
a phlegmy mooring undone below ground,
you're only seed, rankling.
Wheat. Beans. Corn.
They're all the same, aren't they?
Getting gluey in their painful maturing from one,
dribbling neon,
breaking their dormancy
and doing it some harm.
There is a reason to trust, but I can't think of it.
Your pale green flap foams and renders,
not contrite yet.
The muscle strains in its huge, primordial cell-tent.
You look mocked. All this is happening
to you, and you just look wounded,
scalped and pulped.
You're being mortified in an arcane hot light,
and I'm watching you.
The born come remorseless and panging.
The sprout can't answer to the force that feeds him.

KNOTTED, NERVY, ENORMOUS

These roots are like horses' heat: plodding, soured, snug,
whole in earth's trough of sense,
heavy with remains.
A storm has thrust them up and turned them in;
lingering astride,
they are bemused to be on land but different,
have no inkling of what matters now.
Daubed with sand, they're solid, strange:
knotted, nervy, enormous,
hands, tendons, organs amiss. They clot
newborn in lodging mammalian, their future
mysterious, their bulk without mercies,
inclined, astretch,
and the leaves still come from a prone place, shivering out
with minute abandon.
The chase is on: all around
thickets vie, and briars weave in a coming,
toadstools mount upright
until sun-stricken, brown leaves dangle
in a swoon, and the scarlet
change happens, or will happen.
Insects nudge, glistening
with the spat of forage.
But adrift like the dead and not allowed to leave,
beholden to the forest they had made,
the beeches,
tossed wrong by wind, want it
again—want
to go home.

THE LAW

Caterpillars lurch
toward some grand infusion, for what?
For the maw; they *should.*
Luscious, the leaf they snip
with stars in jaws
is so confusing,
a blurt of wellness, their great undoing,
countered in plunder
by these divas
in their daily effort against abundance.
It is lascivious, the law that says
"eat,"
you must, or else—but nobody cares or fights it.
In order not to be eaten,
they eat and can't stop
—like dying but faster,
more voluptuous,
demanding as a new tree
before those who must live.
And so they strain to be just as generous,
distend, let loose their gravy-like stuff
in folds around the object, food,
to secure the thing before its glossiness goes. Capillary
gorge. Accordion flesh
and russet swing, the sheen of the urge to grow.
And their minor head rears,
limbering in air,
and the shy lip leaps out and tears off oak:
a flap and whip of paper
like a sail.
All that bedding in the body bends, the tube
so spotted and hungry
buckles for what comes:
the lunge in an inch
of impossible tree,
holding ground.

QUEEN ANNE'S LACE

She ruined herself in a sort of rumpus,
dizzy with florets.
The brusque little stream dried out,
and she lost her tact, the marvelous
ambivalence of balance. So she fritters
with quanta of insects.
Her wispiness was bred for her mate,
who moons in a meadow with a bitten stalk.
She towers, too shrewd to give up, wants to live
solely for vengeance.
The frilly kerchief of lace steadies her gaze
for what it's worth,
the dark blue brooch
piercing the heart.
Her lyric has been broken. She leans over.

BEES STUMBLE

The old-world machinery of beework
is an arguing with azure odds. The guys land, weave,
grab; headlights go dusty.
Some bees stumble—the knights are drastic. They go to ride.
What you didn't see was the system.
They send a stiff, dark thread down to mine,
stinking, hydraulic,
and withdraw it minutely. The flower throbs,
selfish, quirky. The bourse goes wild,
youngsters yell, cells are cracking,
and the big, mild farmers of our lives
divvy up the take,
harpists, moronic,
left-footed.

PRUNING IN WINTER

Maybe I haven't seen a tree before, unbedded
from its snarl of loveliness.
At fault in winter, it will cringe and swirl,
sucking for months on swaddling air.
I've got to care for it,
rid apple of all blocks to bloom and fruitfulness,
a monk,
a wasp,
my hands welter-weight, knees knitted,
foreign-flecked.
Trees may sharpen me,
aflutter, serrated,
stalky, tall:
so many limbs too tight and full
could batter me,
I'd sicken in the nest
and scratch and pierce
and be pierced back,
rough taste of mingling at a solstice.
If only I were a horse,
I'd know what to do with an orchard.
But I'm less,
a small mark lost in sedge,
a seedless, wind-bearing bulb.
I didn't ask to be set in the middle
of a stark, fast aurora,
was sent here to do a job, be taught,
snap off the halos of overgrown branches
before the apples were born.
His hand slips over me,
rank, teaching,
rasping on the wind, an ashy eking,

yet he knows that work and love should be simple,
and someday they will be.
I would like to stroke the wither of his cheek, the weariness.
God limps. The road's ragged,
last year's weeds have wept their seed, hung on,
and now they are scathed and shattered.
How can I lift my fingers
to the grappling stars of twigs
and cut, and toil, and tender?

BLIGHT IS A FRUIT, TOO

In March, my neighbors
try their thirst by carving bramble
that has chosen them,
a small thing in with earth
on the back roads,
up the houses, fast
in wells,
tiding gates with a dead rush
of lost shoot,
storm of pause where a pheasant can turn.
The thrust was at home with us,
stayed the winter,
and grew immune.
Our muscle of wind is finally the loser
to thorn.
But blight is a fruit, too.
Beginner, it mans thicket, puddle,
binds us, feels
a rolling emptiness, pushes to fill.
Dim red cane nears.
We stab, and try to settle it.

III

BORN

Be planted. Don't do anything to stop it.
Let the woozy wrap around your nonnegotiable hardness
slump and stretch a little. It'll take a few days.
Then your brown snood drops off
and riplets of dry tide, the squirms,
mutters, hiccups, carve
the fey down delightful:
they are sunk, and dark.
Sand can be a lax receiver, but if you're lucky,
a hardy mound will hold you,
unwitted, yet to be trusted,
those mineral courses
impossible to feel or see, but good to think of.
Strum them if you like.
Conduct a chorus of complaint
and groan,
reach, settle, and strive.
Tell the small voices, so abstemious but muscular,
that you will wait until the grand warm-up passes
into lyric, deep song
of always yet to come.
And be playful. They will not want
your wandering baton
or might or measly syllable
if you cannot sound it lightly.
Know that even (or especially)
your foremost wand
as it edges, ogles, and listens, testing ground,
letting loose, getting done,
is a spark's fragment,
a severe fraction
of the strength of tree or flower.

DELPHINIUM

For a few weeks, a streaming
—the only word she can give it—
of everything into her tendril trumpets
at the center of each inky blue tear,
what God has considered blossom.
Who is he? delphinium wants to know,
but too busy with the streaming,
lets it go. She is no maiden,
though her rounded, crisping pores
get shivery at the thought of seeds,
but a wanderer with tender feet.
They are resting now, wan and slim,
in a place of welcome to worms and their brethren,
and the inkling steps they took
are safely behind them.
All day she shimmers, lax and wriggling,
a frilly power in the climbing light
whose rays must touch her or else lose color,
achingly drift,
so all the time she feels the tetchiness of sun
on her curly shoulder.
Her thinness cavils and swells, topping,
looming from each flower cell
in a bead of oozy light,
and the honeybees fondle it
with huge, hairy feet
rushed and doddery.
In luminous delight
the string of beads bunches,
all haem, and soft but ripe,
studding her like hummingbirds tribing at a spring tree,
and the fluttery petals will seem ghostly someday,
an ashy frittering.
But she will know they were her beauty,

her little physical pelt, the tendency
to flower and swarm out
among a million lush and calling creatures
dandled in the light
for the gaze of one who knows them.
Drying herself,
she can still smell a blueness,
pricking at her.
She is intended, she knows, for much else,
the splash of seedlings from her narrowness,
a burst of light when all seems straitened.
Soon, she cannot bend; the brownish stem would snap.
She balances instead,
feeling rather tight,
the lips of finished seeds itching at her.
She is demanded, almost done,
and wonders if the butterfly traveling the place
will even notice her,
the sparrow pause to nibble.
She will return, then,
to the wormy lode beside her feet,
to the politesse
of season and brethren
who have missed her in her blooming.

JUST A CRIMP IN LUSHNESS

Worms have no minds,
so we say. Just a crimp
in lushness,

the inking of passion
in mucus
and soil. Maybe they

can't see, because
there is no sign.
They squeeze into darkness

and make it their own,
baring the way,
hungry for honest work,

and the resounding humus
rises in them easily,
ready again to enter,

unable to stay.
Their job is mongering
in leavings, being called by

the insignificant:
the little wet lair that rises
out of nothing

in a yard,
seeks their flutter,
takes their rhythm,

needs them,
and they live with it.
But everything's brief,

the body shirks
as it mingles,
sinks, idles,

and lastly refrains.
Earth is no different,
and there is no reason

in any of this
to make sense of what matters—
the comedown of deepness

under us
is so sudden, simple,
harmless.

CONGREGATING

Tomatoes were made for this: a loud, fierce sucking.
Word gets around. Whiteflies
come drubbing.
They're beating on pulp with sloshy-flaked feelers
sneaking blood
and fruit slops them silly
with dunked hallelujahs.
There's a scandal deep down
where seeds swirl golden
as larvae—
it's an opera, no keeping
of aria for next time.
And no sermon.
Weed fields are flighty. Tomatoes are rotting.
Glom on.
In voices thin as children's, they scream *savior*
and squeeze red rainbow.

NOON

Horses are tugging some spoor of green
down to the center
under hot sun,
a blessing like the longing begun,
lowering of light in a moan made soft.
Fetlocks are bobbing
in a little fit
of rhythm;
balm in noses wrinkles,
settles,
wrinkles.
Noon is blameless.
Afield, horses link in dwelling
long in fescue
of a hummock,
cornered in alfalfa's blue spurts.
Juices stain the dark
down into herbivore
alive
with a green threading fences and lots.
There is no need to be beautiful
so long as there is another need:
to be heavy-hoofed, say,
clopping a deep sway of nettle
without fierce feeling.
It is all right to be armless
if the long curtain of body
swells in daylight,
pursed and glossy.
It is all right to have no alertness
if hairs cover you slowly in deep dun
that leans in and covets only you.
It is fine to be a monotone

delicious in the same sound
that faints like a power
in the sun.
And it is a wonder, the smell of manger
taken out to paddock,
lit slowly from within
as animals are—
in the meadow of noon
before night can come
when all old things just are.

MOUSE HISTORY

They are winging over me
so politely,
this interested, separate species.
Unction ghosts their feet
with possibility
and spreads to me
with divine weight, a bobbing might
as they run this fine,
fine course
of curiosity
treading an unseen, airy loop of light.
No problem. Union. Communion. A rout
by mouse of human
willing, like a tale of what can be:
they peel forward on their feet
up my arm to the shoulder,
roost at the neck,
and breathe delirious, dainty puffs
at the ear,
alarming and fortuitous flower.
Their floss is my might
or could it be?
My cardigan loses their delicate steps, a rival
in subtlety.
This is legal, isn't it?
Mice all over me,
a royal family of souls
gone far,
gone right,
so slight on their feet,
their thinking feet,
pausing only to skid and restore,
angels at the shrinking edge and unafraid,

whirling down,
kneading a forearm's puny hairs
and doing everything again.
They're maestros
of what is modest and certain,
and I'm claiming kin,
feeling quibbles, purges, and such swift lulls
of temperature
and intelligence.
This is species mingling,
though who would believe it?
Well, I'm ten
and I can
and I also can believe
that mice are writing their lives
lightly on my shoulder, on my forehead
with such decorum,
in the slippery pores of sweater, in the little learning
that embalms me,
in my wild mildness of skin.

MY BELUGAS

They lower themselves lordly,
the pluming old revelers.

My belugas dangle blond
in submerged jubilance

citrus-like with slickness
of the Saguenay

or St. Lawrence rivers,
lured as if by spine

down into the swivel
of slipshod French sound.

Their form? Albino aubergine
forgetfulness. Loopily they fan

and turn the tallow of horizon
with the arching lushness

of unheeding fern,
twiddle their cloven tail fins

a little looser all evening.
The thick white crayon

of him curving strains
against the pouting currents,

nooks of cursive granite,
and a sun that pops

and percolates.
Then alone

milky whale reconsiders,
creaks and sings

his slow, lit exuberance.
Poisson, poisson,

he coughs
to her,

upside down.

ABSOLUTION

I envy the sun
his touch on your skin
and your thanklessness to him,
the alarm
as calm meets calm incandescent
and you accept his heat
without noticing it, bend in
just slightly
to touch some innerness he wakens.
You say there is no absolution
and you can give me none.
But there is heat, a steadiness,
a swelling clime unmembering us.
Blood's the problem.
It sings a spiritual of no sense,
a percussive and persuasive losing.
I am alone, and my blood beats,
and yours does.
The sun has no such secret.
I have seen light bear down on sprouts
too singular and weak to resist. That's absolution:
the feeling of being
when something is poured into one.

WOLF MATE

Bloody my mouth, for I have bitten you—my prey idle and lush,
    with fur that ruffles your jaw. Little that you know,
I love that little with my cave,
          my tongue,
the winter's foul,
   hybrid hive.
Don't say ice doesn't seethe, too. Recall
    the mound of paw clutching roughened and wild
under shaken snow,
    tiding, raw, and rested
      where my lank February body sinks
  before my return to you.
I eat only stubs; I feel
    a muck in the wound. I wish instead
      that I could be a cloud
and believe that I may have done all I can to become.
         Sooty arboreal ooze
flutters in the air as if all the family
   has starved by now
  and nothing will happen hereafter.
     Yet doubt keeps me alert.
   I seek debris—the promise
         of a mountaintop that never
     could rise for me,
turret rock, humus home,
  a stranded comet
cold from the lick of me. Your blood could not
    ever meet mine.
Still I arch, stink of sage,
    and insist you lodge. Your blood
  brightens me.

CLEMATIS

All the others have gone home,
but she is his home.
There is no holding him except
in her open purpling lobe,
the frontal fringe
and speckling of paleness
down toward loam:
a giant ruffle
of the egregiously blue
and willingly cream,
she is all steady lunging
in moonlight.
He can't help but notice
clematis still blooming in darkness,
swelling in simple praise
from petal to cloud.
She bides on the fence.
All nervousness, he panders and waits,
his cleft ridge tidy with green jewels
that tipple with the stars;
his tired feet flickering as they must
on the direct tap of night
and the bar of gate;
his ankling lust.
It is too much to bear to love with sight,
so we must close our eyes. He does.
The waft of her is weight. Her bloominess is fluff.
He patters on her, pestles all her mereness,
stuffs it in himself,
molders, wobbles, feels sick,
and lights off
for another outer rim of shining darkness.

HONEYSUCKLE

Tongue in honeysuckle,
I am dripping,
tasting the true tendril
inked gently
—sweet touch, such bilge
of cosmos rising up from the curly length
that ties the woods together loosely,
longing for largeness in sump.
Sap sprawls.
I'm tickled in a thin green tide
of honey,
sucking on the strings of a song.

DEFLOWERING

Deflowering is the wrong word,
wrong in so many ways.
He will not take anything away
that you wanted to keep
if you have chosen him.
Instead, he is going to find
the flower.
It is busy work,
and he will be busy at it,
but so should you be,
angling in your singularity
to find a way out of it.
You might suggest to him, *this*
or *that,*
feel me. Better.
Neither of you knows what you are doing
looking for this thing,
this feeling,
a legend.
But he is also a feeling
and a legend,
and there is no flower
unless he is one.
You will have to find him,
and though he may seem evident
—even, distastefully obvious—
he isn't.
His flower, like yours,
is in abeyance,
hanging back, a touch ingrown,
because he has been waiting for too long
for you to find it.
So be stealthy;

this is a tender secret
that will not pass from you.
And when you find
what you need to know of him,
you must turn back
and look once more for you.
Do not assume anything;
nothing is only yours
since him.
His own, too, he must know again,
and this may take some time
after your touch on him.
You are not alone, and yet
the two of you are not one
exactly, there is so much to do
as more and more flowers find you.
But it is not about flowers, is it?
It is above and under
all words.

IV

ARCHAIC CORN

> *During the annual rituals honoring Osiris,*
> *the ancient Egyptians fashioned small "mummies"*
> *from a mixture of clay, sand, and grains of corn...*
> *The Egyptians considered corn a living element of*
> *a natural cycle embodying the concept of resurrection*
> *and renewal.*
>
> —The Brooklyn Museum

A beam of dawn loomed into a ridge of supple beads,
    raised like a froth, maize braiding us
to old centuries, then cooled and formed
    as though survival were an artifact
and love but a token. Light is a luxury, a burn.
    I milled, I moped, sheer,
askew, a slave in heart,
    underworked agrarian assistant to a man
with a Chicago corner plot
    thick in seethe of sun:
I hoed and scathed a row for him
    of primeval corn.
Doctor So-and-So, a botanist, archaic in
    his rickety stroll and ancient bloom,
bare-ankled as a king,
    was breeding heat and plant back and back
to corn's first self, a genie of our food
    only half a foot tall,
tasselled like a toy but firm
    as bone or copse—
the stalk a flight of genes across
    the scars of lakes that burrowed in
as Nubians glided, gleaned,
    plucked a rattling abacus,
their lozenged words clenching a dignity
    never since heard,
beseeching a lunar god to balm,
    tonguing the trace of iron
in a word, with edges dyed in umber

like some riot of the earth.
Their scrawl of sound bequeathed a sign,
    could not betray anyone,
the doubt pounded in so it could last
    despite its scream. I long
for the precise, dry
    satiety of their stance, the rivulet
of what was known, progress
    of a blaze in sound, and for the way a workman's hand
brought itself justly to the task of making.
    In that language of angular stillness
no blurt went unobserved, the grammar
    was frank, remorseless.
We gaze at the bulging knees
    of Assyrian warriors poised in fragments,
upon the calm pulse of a sting at labor
    on the wall of stone: no shiver
not heeded, no pain foregone,
    each thwarting now a presence.
The severity—thrust, throw—of the fighter
    and the artist is certain as if steamed
by a sun passing over oceans, orchards,
    a mind as it flowers and flames.
The resolute queens stir what they can of their thoughts
    in molten vessels, and servants
do this work in their stead
    when the mistresses must dream—dawdle a way
after crickets who hop for heaven,
    then choose to return to a normal life.
I defer to all of those who loiter,
    who may not change or vary,
beloved by the shroud of our sun
    as by the seemly relic that loved the small corn
before it bled into Illinois.
    Those harsh beings had a reign.
Yet my archaic master ailed without me,
    surrounded in his city by his kernels and straws.
I fled the beating language,
    the curse of growth, sultriness,
the corn's strange harvests.

DREAM OF HYDRANGEA

I've dreamed of hydrangea:
the shrub like a Victorian childhood,
full and ominous in its beliefs.

There is no pressing past that embrace
the plant makes of itself;
broad leaves are complete
in the darkness they guide.

Spots on the green,
how they yellow in heat,
are the signs of something latent.

The flower is the token.
Looming and odorous,
Viennese in comely conceit,
the loot is deep, deep blue—

The threat of heaven
when you don't want it,
or the coming to earth
of a moon
in shoes.

ALL THAT HANKERING

Your heavy plaits of what I cannot
tweak or pinch but mar it
is the virus more than virus, golden Epsom of desire
sagging on an untoward stem.
I can't read or speak "sunflower,"
have to grasp it with the fogged blush of kin.

       ***

How did you twirl your leaves out?
Now they're browning, caught in a wind
that blows the summer off.
What an undertaking,
your crude burst from a rut
where seed was flung, learned,
then all that hankering in a flowering crowd for sun,
the oily scale
of your huge raincoat skin.
How did you learn to hurry?
And how did you find patience?
It was sown in the ground
where we each bury
a disturbance.

       ***

Trust me, said the wind
to the big buds waiting to happen,
uncertain of what stalk was meant for
and what bitterness awaited. Trust me. I am the master
and orbit your skin
until the smallish suns in there grow restless
for more stuff, extrude, get wild with self
and rush into bloom.

***

Your flowering is not like the others,
it seems so hasty and gigantic, probably vulgar.
The gang feels no hitch at all in anything.
But your leader may boggle
at the jangled ground, and seethe a little
honey through her pores, packed,
boxed, blessed
with hardiness and mist of sun.

***

The tide you stir is ragged,
lunging, full of patriotism
for the soon undone,
a pastiche of the spent and flourishing.
Your rending causes pride, and should.
The stalks glisten and gag
on age, time. The rhythm's a flutter
on top as enormous eyes
open in roughed-up faces
and drop their eager breaths
in a tide of untaught pollen.

***

Your litter is raw,
bent as if slashed,
the current hushed and soughed.
Pellets bead your smile; you are tired.
But a power purges you tough ghosts,
sapped to become more yourselves—
crisp, salty, known.
Your dust is tossed
of sky and ground;
it rises up from crevasse
to soothe and end
in caress
your emptying strut.

PINE BARRENS

I'm a pilgrim frugging in the locks of resin
that embarrass the bark,
thwarting a bureaucracy of phloem,
the up-and-down paternoster drift.
Gum isn't salve for hardship,
it's tough slime to harry the tree with.
I should know such a worsening.
Travail is not slight, it sickens
pores of pain around with rime,
an unseen glistening.
I was wronged, I resist, the coarsening is too much—
I am crossed, caught
in the prowess of distrust.
Barbaric, flamboyant, I float in pus.

NONE OF US CAN SWIM

Chamomile, mullein leaf, rose hip:
a stealth sandpapers sense.
I don't believe in health.
Dreamy nosegays, the kid-whine
of "healing" herbs—none of us can swim.
The cure's a case of nerves,
a toy book propped up on a hairy leaf,
an abrupt wilt.

SPECIES FEVER

I like to sit and watch lizards, at length,
but we can't live together,
so they are under the heat lamp,

purple and shrouded,
and they persist.
Their feet were forgiven much earlier

when there was much to forgive;
they've clambered and scattered into this era.
No one is chiding them now.

Think, after all, of the family:
their long, rusticated bodies
on the big false twig,

languorous and alert;
look at the lustrous
dry tails, level,

without a twitch;
see how the wrinkles ride the ribs
from the edge,

lovely curls somehow caught
in a sapient crunch
and left to hanker

for the skeleton;
and look, above all, at the fingers.
They are not unlike our clever new wands,

making placements insatiably,
and yet left at a loss
with idleness.

But theirs are always idle,
never ignorant—they are so decorous.
The narrow ribbon of feeling flickers between;

the large eyelids hover,
drop shut under the healing lamp,
and the well-worked skin

scales these small continents,
aging with them in species fever.
A bruise in the elder's armpit

is a badge of pain
and a portent,
and the younger ones sniff it.

Their thighs are natty, though thin,
and there is much mildness
in the sudden family bond.

A memory of time before
time enchants them, scurvy as they are,
intent on those millipedes,

and willing to snap off
the ends of each other's tails.
It is not unfriendly, their binge and probe,

it is just family
left on a precipice
late in the century.

REVERIE OF LEAF MOLD

In the Talmage woods, the path is spent,
and the groundhog squats on his hillock, fatter than it,
hot-faced, fang dowdy,
shag to wobble,

and if a groundhog dreams
near a mown field, big to his fate,
forgetting all the tunnels,
then summer has ended.

Down the road, a geranium dump undoes itself deeper,
minding humus stranded,
petals gone limp in the earthen dark;

dark covets, parsimonious with pleasure,
wrecking it with dank
and ether: that's rot,
giddy shamble, a lump.

Trucked in and shaken down a ramp once,
the marred flowers were wrought by light

but now, lit from underneath the gloom of oak
by larvae, damp pulse,
to them the feeling of a sidling life
is unguent, unbidden,

and the salving goes on
without merit or pause
in the small roots, a probing,

a voice of pleasure and stealth,

dawnishness,
a death;

and that is why the ground that rises
to meet an animal full in the haunch can be trusted—

it will let the animal rest
and rest,

then moisten him, a fruit
in the dark,

an endless passing.

FURTIVE AND FIERY

A flame skittered from your rough center
before you had to swish and drop it.
I look at zinnias, molting brown,
roused by lastness to show a violence.
They lived inside themselves
with exigence for too long,
furtive and fiery—
purples without real longing,
just grave sashay and goodbye,
yellows mugging for survival, pinks
bopping with belief before.
I admire the curlicues of a damp self
about to buckle,
the shake of the head,
the knotted vegetable matter,
the greenish festoons of fiber
dense, astray
in deciduous caves.

AN END OF IT

When a bear comes out at last into the woods
there is a snagging smell, the taste
of something sour in the air about him. It is sap.
It surrounds him. That's what he knows.
The tangy and revolting stuff
is stuck to trees he would have overlooked
before this spring,
this beastly longing.
The bear, he lumbers, they say,
yet really he is just remembering,
remembering the sweetish lumps of larger animals
not with him now
as he goes wandering.
But their smell is with him, their earnest, sordid smell,
once ticklishly embalming,
a pleasure
like rank peaches just before
they slip open. Arms of the firs are trembling.
Stacked on the mountain, they seem
like overwintered homes for ghosts.
He cannot, after all, keep living
where he has stashed himself
these many months,
cryptic and coalesced,
remote and slightly moldering.
Though he loves lankness,
dried mud behind rock,
the scattering of seeds
and rootish hulks inside
his hiding place, he reached
an end of it.

EGRET

The slick head has seamed the bay
and trusted in.
True rhythm is that water, sunken ripple
underseen.

V

ARCHAEOPTERYX

Scientists have found the fossil remains
of a reptile-like bird that lived about
125,000,000 years ago. This bird is called
Archaeopteryx, which means ancient one with wings.

—*The World Book Encyclopedia*

For those who would rather not be reminded
of hip bone, bare coccyx, pommel grip of shoulder,
grillework of chance rib, the deserted architecture,
for them it will not figure that the mind, and the heart,
are a slickness in our body's cirrus
and must slip out.
Dreaming is my bed, a banned seed in portage,
the gooey horsehair virus
of want and stop
lost in a canal's fickle lining—
and if too fickle, then my dreaming
is of dryness.
Ponds clot a town
of rueless feather beds,
massed floating mattresses,
and rancorous deep springs,
embodied, open-ended comforts,
where the coffee always comes with a fat puff of milk,
where the pancakes are as wide as the sun.
I tended an inseparable self,
tapped out a likeness on a steep butte.
The cipher of my vim is meant to mystify.
A fossil bird, I have slept.

FOSSIL KNOWLEDGE

The lavishness is what I'd criticize
if I knew the artist—

flecks of id and blunder
pencilled on a rock

before I lived.
Yet now I study it,

stricken in my moment
and almost bereft,

read from the tablet how moss
overspent the phylum,

strewing dry capsules.
Pleistocene catfish

gave up its shadow intact
to darkness,

its soul a garbage.
Death seemed to bless the smaller fish:

animal as exact stalk
inked in eon

on gathered slate
and never minded.

I wonder what the fish could have told me
of itself, its climax—

small brain torrid
in a polar lock;

bottom bloom smartly suckered;
worthy spine

stroked, shattered, recorded.
They were all misbegotten

on short notice,
thrived if they could,

and left a message
of fin and sperm

avowed,
effervesced:

pocks, limned,
tilted vitals mocked by a fantasy rain,

nebulae of swamp frothy, halted;
ruin just contained

in a scribble-scrabble
on a flat stone.

BONDAGE

After a bad night,
Goya might have invented turkeys.

Almost swamped by ink,
with squishy combs and martian gizzards,

they muddle and intrigue out back in the shade,
pendulous compared with chickens, and listless,

squatting like big buds and carrying on
with royal elongations when they choose to walk.

None of it seems needed, a forced retirement
of mavens, money-makers,

stars with silk skins riven,
all besotted,

who knew what elegance is
and now must mimic it—

legs losing ground before some secret urge
and shimmying; slavish bowing

of bulbous ends;
sloping fronts huge and quivering

in a sham of decorum;
face a tattered sag

studded by a slipshod fantasy eye
like a signet ring.

When they kneel to rest, turkeys always lose face.
The ruddy sling that knots their heads in bondage

clogs, stirs, loosens,
lets the beak down to jut

weak and glistening with barnyard acne,
and a piece of flesh drips from the dart

and doodles pinkly, heavy bag.
Raw, the old eye courts and wanders.

They need an impresario; they need a folklore.
They need religious relics,

laws for order and governance,
and grandiose titular gatherings

of scions with copper-colored crowns
and rending contraltos.

These they will not have.
Next door, the chicken tribe stoops and paws,

perambulating with a purpose,
chests pecked, bared, fouled

by rivals or friends.
Oh golden twitch, the cock in charge

minces and carols—the court is in the pen
and no wiser.

Glum under beeches,
turkeys nod and lunch, twist and lour

in fits and starts of oral hysteria,
as if former subjects were harrowing them

with good gossip,
snips and dabs of heaven they are missing.

JANUARY CALM

When wolves meet,
much is already understood:
a lingering catness,
troubled in the lope;
the abraded tuft,
scattered and jostling muscle;
a long link of grassy knowledge unforetold.
The breath of wolf is indrawn, not puffed,
a brawny lack,
his softness in pursuit
so unconceived and unencumbered,
it is almost chance
or mishap. Who wants to know
what he has not heard of?
It is said they know
what they want—
in fact, they want nothing
and are no one,
the fur's desire informal
like something sparked, then blown out.
Lust and light belong to a younger body of creature,
and the sidestepping arrogance of hunter
comes from a dream of deep earth
where hunger is unharried, never quenched.
The kin of yellow tooth
and incognizant, sensitive
lunge and abandon
aren't present to themselves
except as a fleeting remedy.
Their neural friendship is a sigh,
the love a cold fidelity
not to persist or be chosen,
the vibrancy of ear springs in response

to a nothing,
the ice soprano of nothing.
We are what we fear.
The little nervous wolf-brat
feels fast, half-made, unresilient,
"free,"
and worries. His nappy worsted coat sways
with the ghost of meadow,
infirm cue of what is north.
The stealth from which he was fashioned
is a mistake,
as it is a mistake that he gnaws his own wound,
unable to mother hurt.
I can't love myself in pain,
neither can you.
He nicks his mind on a cloud;
the nights grow stiff.
He secretes a January calm.
The family crouches, decides to forego
the prey near at hand.
Instead they will spray across the plains to find
a body they long for
as their own.

Molly McQuade's poetry has appeared in *The Paris Review,*
The American Scholar, North American Review, Pequod, and elsewhere.
Her writing has received fellowships and awards from the New York
Foundation for the Arts, the Pew Charitable Trusts, PEN, the National
Council of Teachers of English, and the Illinois Arts Council. Her
poetry also received New York University's Philo and Sally Higley
Award. McQuade served as poetry columnist for *The Hungry Mind
Review* and previously founded and edited the poetry review column
of *Publishers Weekly*. Her poetry criticism has also been published in
The Washington Post and *Newsday,* among others. Currently she is a
contributing editor for Graywolf Press, a correspondent for *Booklist,*
and a board member of the National Book Critics Circle. A collection
of her essays about poetry, *Stealing Glimpses,* was published by
Sarabande Books in 1999. She has also edited *By Herself,* an
anthology of essays about poetry, released by Graywolf Press in 2000.